VON ELIJAH Presents:

HOW TO GET A RAISE OR PROMOTION SIMPLIFIED

Do you want a raise?
Tired of getting overlooked for promotions?

KEEON RUDDER

HOW TO GET A RAISE OR PROMOTION SIMPLIFIED
by Keeon Rudder

Published by CreateSpace
4900 Lacross Rd
North Charleston, SC 29406
(843) 789-5000

CreateSpace is a registered trademark
of On-Demand Publishing, LLC

Cover design by Jared Williams
and his firm at *DooglesCreativeSolutions.com*

June 2016:   First Edition

While every precaution has been taken in the preparation of this book, the publisher and author assume zero responsibility for errors, omissions, or for damages resulting from the use of the information contained herein.

ISBN-13: 978-1530629534
ISBN-10: 1530629535

Dedication

To my loving, intelligent, and thoughtful sister.

Shevon Quijano, you have been a blessing to many people.

Your character emanates Christ daily via all that you do and say.

Thank you for your prayers, support, and words of encouragement.

I pray God grants you and your family excellent health,

and all of the desires of your heart.

VE

VON ELIJAH

In Loving Memory of

Dan Oren Dinges, Jr., Marcus Deon Henderson,
Mavis Emelia Noel, Stephanie Rena Riley,
and Sandra Debra Fair

Much sweat, much pay – Less sweat, less pay.

—Auliq Ice

Contents

HOW TO GET A RAISE OR PROMOTION SIMPLIFIED

Introduction

Raises and promotions are rarely easy subjects to discuss. The topic of money—period—has the power to make anyone feel uncomfortable and uneasy.

Many employees downright fear their yearly performance reviews. Others dislike confrontation so they squeamishly walk on pins and needles when they negotiate their raises so as not to appear confrontational. Simply put, negotiating pay raises and asking for promotions can be extremely scary and unnerving.

Almost every employee has questions in regards to earning a raise or promotion:

- How do I prove I deserve a raise or a promotion?
- How much money should I ask for?
- Will the boss demote or fire me if I ask for more money?
- How often should I ask for a raise?
- Does my salary accurately reflect my worth?
- How much are my peers in the same field making with similar work experience?

Æ Are money and time-off my only negotiating tools?

Æ Can we just negotiate my salary bump over text messages so I don't have to sit across from my boss?

Æ Can I hire an attorney for a few hours and let them negotiate my promotion?

Æ What if my boss says 'No'?

Æ Why can't employees just receive automatic, predetermined raises every year?

Æ Can I get my wife or brother-in-law to sit in for me during my yearly performance review?

Employers often times do not explicitly tell their employees what they need to do in order to earn raises and promotions. Some employers frequently tell their staff that the company does not have the money or available resources to give raises, while corporate expenditures paint a different picture to employees. This can leave many employees feeling clueless or intrusive when they navigate the promotion waters.

Employees, on the other hand, sometimes errantly believe hard work, team work, punctuality, and cheerfulness in the workplace will guarantee themselves advancement. Still other employees are under the impression that their tenure with the company should automatically warrant a raise or promotion.

When employers and employees' expectations—often times not clearly communicated if at all—are not met, that can lead to resentment, a decrease in morale, transfers, and even termination.

Hopefully, this simple story will pacify your uncertainty and allow you to peaceably reach your goals. The company Paige Story works for is not real, although the situations she faces are quite relevant today. Information about her company was purposefully omitted from this story in order to leave it nameless and faceless. This approach, hopefully, will make it easier for you to consider these situations and principles when thinking about your own company.

NOW is *your* time to move up in your company and grab firm control of your career trajectory. Read this book in its entirety to find out how.

Chapter 1
Not Today, Any Day but Today

To escape fear, you have to go through it, not around.
—Richie Norton

You'll earn more money doing something you love, rather than just doing something because it pays you a high salary.
—Auliq Ice

A cool breeze blew through the cracked four panel window. "What on earth was I thinking staying out so late last night?" Paige moaned as she sleepily rolled over, forcefully willing her right arm from underneath the blanket to hit the snooze button on her phone.

Today was the dreaded day. If it was within her power, she would give an entire month's paycheck to skip this day every year.

Paige had been with the company for eight years but received a pay raise only once. As the years piled up she felt less appreciated and began to hate her yearly performance reviews. She felt that her tenure warranted a promotion but she wasn't quite sure how to ask for a raise.

She did the best she could with the little information that she had. She read countless articles about acquiring raises but found them to be quite frustrating. She discovered that most publications about asking for raises focused—almost exclusively—on things she should not do or say. Instead, she wanted to be proactive, but few articles that she read satisfied that longing.

The little information that she did find useful typically pertained to negotiation techniques that turned her yearly performance review into something resembling a Roman gladiator spectacle. She hated confrontation and avoided it at all cost, but she felt like she was forced to argue her points in order to prove her worth at the company.

Every year she would have a panic attack that intensified as her performance review inched closer. During her performance reviews she would sweat profusely and retreat to her invisible shell praying the torture would end quickly.

As the years piled up, she avoided confrontation by accepting her boss's first offer. His negotiation ploy frustrated her all the more when he claimed the company did not have the money to give her the raise she deserved. He promised to take care of her as soon as things turned around, which seemed less and less likely with every passing year.

Paige frequently asked for help and tried the advice given to her, but unfortunately did not get the results she sought. She was fed-up with the entire process and if it was up to her, she would call in sick on days that she had scheduled performance reviews.

Paige was a fantastic worker. She was well liked and got along with her co-workers and superiors, and was generally considered congenial with a pleasant demeanor and a sharp wit, which made her a hoot to be around. She had no trouble connecting with the women in the office, often being complimented on her fashion sense and even giving them tips on where to find similar clothing and accessories. The men in her office also enjoyed chatting with her as she possessed an endearing knowledge of football and basketball, and could easily banter with the best of them.

She was a fast learner and jack-of-all-trades who was quick to grasp the nuances of her co-workers' roles. She was also known to be a patient teacher who cheerfully accepted the additional responsibility of acclimating recent hires to the requirements of their job descriptions.

Paige was an office standout by any stretch of the imagination. Her professionalism, work experience, friendliness, punctuality, and drive made her both likeable and resourceful. She simply lacked confidence in relaying her merits to her boss during her yearly performance reviews.

As she hopped out of the shower wrapped in her dark green cotton bath robe, she groggily scanned her undersized closet to figure out what she wanted to wear. She started with shoes and systematically browsed through her tops, blouses, jeans, pantsuits, and skirt suits to complete her ensemble. Finally, she settled on a neon blue crochet dress, which was comfortable and low maintenance to reflect her melancholy. She snapped on a few pieces of oversized jewelry, put on a light coat of makeup, and slipped out the front door.

Fifteen minutes later, she arrived to work just as the second hand on her watch landed on 7:00 a.m. Out of breath, she stepped out of the elevator and as she rounded the corner to her desk, saw five co-workers huddled together with looks of bewilderment on their faces.

Paige set her beige baguette purse down on her desk and moseyed her way over to the group. Her mind was racing trying desperately to figure out if the group was upset with her for some reason. She played back the events of the prior week in her mind to see if she had done or said something egregious to any of her co-workers.

As she inched closer to the group, Ashley lunged forward, grabbed Paige by the arm and pulled her into the circle to give her the scoop. Paige felt her body temperature immediately rise as she tried to remember if she put on deodorant before leaving her house.

Before Ashley could open her mouth, Morales interrupted and asked Paige, "Did you hear what happened to Ty Collier?"

"Ssshhhh…" Kelsey said with a look of disapproval. "Not so loud, blabber mouth."

"Ah, who cares? It's not like he's going to be here tomorrow to punish us is he?" Richard chimed in.

With eyes still fixated on Paige, Ashley continued, "Ty up and quit over the weekend and nobody knows why."

"Are y'all sure he did not get fired because that guy was a total tool?" Richard pushed a stack of papers to the side and plopped his behind on the desk.

"No," Kelsey matter-of-factly retorted. "I am certain Willie—the Janitor—said he heard that Ty quit."

"Yeah, but it's Willie. Even on a good day, you can only make out every other word the man says." Richard folded his arms as he fired back.

The only thing that resonated with Paige was the fact that she would not have to endure that dreadful performance review scheduled for today. She could care less whether her boss Ty quit, got fired, took a Sabbatical, or joined the witness protection program.

"Oh my gosh"—Paige cheered—"this is awesome news!"

Everyone turned at once to look at Paige and waited for her to explain why she was so elated. They figured she was not Ty's number one fan, but she had never bashed him before.

"Don't you see? I don't have to sit in that gosh-awful performance review today! Oh glorious day!" Paige pumped her fists in the air.

As soon as the last word escaped her mouth, in walked someone who had the appearance of a supervisor. Paige's smile quickly vanished as the small group dispersed.

Fear incapacitated Paige as she sat motionless at her desk. Her mind drifted far away from her to-do-list for the day as she maneuvered through the five stages of grief.

In her isolation, her frustration grew at the thought of her co-workers who had bypassed her for promotions. She then bargained with her maker that if today's performance review would be postponed for another time, she would give up her go-to stress reliever, chocolate, for an entire year—or at least six days. Meanwhile, depression quickly set in and amplified her desire for that very thing. Paige reached into the lower compartment of her desk to search for an edible solution for her chocolate fix, but the wrappers were all empty.

As her heart beat slowly increased its pace, she reasoned to herself that maybe, just maybe, she was not actually ready for a promotion. Perhaps this was fate whispering to her that her current position was as far as she would go for the rest of her life.

"Hello. I am Bryan Hynson—the interim supervisor. I don't think we've met."

"Nice to meet you Mr. Hynson." Paige mumbled as she frantically gathered herself. She discreetly wiped the tears from her eyes with her sleeve and extended her clammy hand until it rested firmly in Bryan's palm.

"I saw on Ty's calendar that you two had a performance review scheduled for 10 am today. Let's say we meet in the conference room in fifteen minutes?" Bryan warmly smiled as he returned his hand into his pants pocket.

"Okay," she said, clearing her throat, held together by a paltry emotional string as she tried hard to keep from falling apart in front of him.

"Perfect. See you in a few." Bryan did an about-face and walked away.

HELPFUL TIPS:

- Watch my favorite motivation video *How Bad Do You Want It?* (https://youtu.be/lsSC2vx7zFQ).
- Do not be afraid to make mistakes. Take educated risks. Assess the results. Take more educated risks. Assess those results.

SUMMARY NOTES:

1. Asking for a raise or a promotion can be very scary. Some people get panic attacks or get agitated at just the thought of performance reviews.
2. Many employees hate confrontation and often accept the first offer presented to them.
3. Do not fear!! This book will teach you exactly what you need to do to secure more raises and promotions.

Chapter 2

Little Ms. Chatter Box

The art of conversation is the art of hearing as well as being heard.
—William Hazlitt

Paige hesitantly walked into the conference room. Bryan stood up to again shake her hand. She was far too emotional during their first encounter to pay close attention to Bryan's features. At 5'4" she towered over no one except children but when she stood next to Bryan, she had to look down slightly in order to make eye contact. He wore a tailored grey striped suit accompanied by a light pink dress shirt, with a pink tie featuring grey diagonal strips, a brown belt, and polished brown shoes. Despite his stature, she thought, Bryan was a handsome, well-dressed man.

She sat opposite of Bryan at the oval table. He opened a leather folder that stored a notepad, some loose papers, two pens, and a few business cards. He removed a silver pen and two sheets of paper that were stapled together. He pushed his chair back, crossed his legs, clasped his hands then placed them in his lap, and asked her to tell him a little about herself.

Bryan attentively listened as Paige glazed over her close relationship with her Grandpa Bill, her childhood, and her collegiate experiences. She respectfully got Bryan caught up on her previous failures to obtain consistent raises or promotions, and then briefly recounted some of the research on the subject that she completed over the years along with the strategies that she attempted to implement during her previous performance reviews in hopes of changing her situation.

Paige also did a fantastic job of asking Bryan a few ice-breaker questions as well. Through the use of open-ended and follow-up questions they ping ponged the conversation back and forth, each person locked in and totally engaged with what the other had to say.

As the meeting drew to a close, Paige felt good about their engaging conversation until she noticed that they had not talked about her job performance at all. Her blood pressure skyrocketed as did her anxiety.

"Don't you want to know why I think I should get a raise?" she blurted out, and then braced herself for the worst.

"Paige, you are absolutely wonderful, so let me tell you what I will do for you. Let's meet every Wednesday after lunch for one hour for the next five weeks and I will teach you some tricks of the trade that will help you earn raises and promotions more regularly." Bryan closed his folder and stood up.

Confusion and disappointment flushed out the joy in her spirit. Discouraged at how her performance meeting ended, she replied, "Sure, I guess that will work."

HELPFUL TIPS:

- Read the book *BRAG! The Art of Tooting Your Own Horn Without Blowing It* by Peggy Klaus to learn how to effectively and succinctly introduce yourself to others.

- Watch the YouTube motivation video *Change* (https://youtu.be/_aAA9-edO3I).

SUMMARY NOTES:

1. There are zero shortcuts to getting a raise or a promotion. Bryan saw that Paige was friendly, well spoken, a hard worker, and loyal to the company. Bryan knew that each of the aforementioned attributes play an integral role when managers decide who to give raises and promotions, but he also believed there are additional factors that can help Paige accomplish her goal.

Chapter 3

Some Battles are Won Before They Begin

I've always considered myself to be just average talent and
what I have is a ridiculous insane obsessiveness
for practice and preparation.
—Will Smith

Most great people have attained their greatest success
just one step beyond their greatest failure.
—Napoleon Hill

The following Wednesday, Paige and Bryan met in the conference room after Paige returned from her lunch break.

"How's your day and week going thus far?" Bryan opened his leather folder.

"Not too bad," Paige cheerfully responded. "But I'm a bit nervous about my meetings with you if I can be 100% honest. Don't get me wrong, I am very appreciative of your mentorship. I'm just nervous that's all."

"Aw, no need to be nervous. I won't yell or scream and I haven't bitten anyone at work in well over a decade," he quipped, laughing faintly. "That was a joke I promise."

Paige smiled and asked Bryan why he carried that leather folder with him to meetings.

Bryan thought for a moment. "A leather folder is both professional and practical for meetings, interviews, and performance reviews. I can store pens, take notes on my notepad, and file papers for quick retrieval. As a matter of fact, I think it would be a good idea for you to get one for yourself, although I won't actually explain why until our third meeting."

He then reached into his folder, tore two blank sheets of paper from his notepad, pulled out a pen, and handed them to Paige. He then removed two pages that had been stapled together for himself. Paige recognized the paper from their first meeting.

At the top of the paper were the words boldly typed *TOPICS FOR MEETING ONE* in bold script.

"We only have two things to discuss today." Bryan pushed his chair back a few inches and settled himself comfortably. Paige followed suit and settled in for their meeting.

"First, please write down your goals in regards to raises and promotions." Bryan paused to give her time to write.

"Really, what for?" Paige's eyes squinted to reveal her confusion.

Bryan then went on to described a 1979 Harvard MBA program study that proved the importance of writing down your goals. Ten years after the students from the study graduated, a follow-up interview showed that the 13% of the class who had goals but did not write them down, on average, was making twice as much as the 84% of students who did not have goals at all. Conversely, the 3% who had clear written goals were earning, on average, ten times as much as the other 97% of students put together.[1]

"Do you know how to quantify your goals?" asked Bryan.
"I think so," she replied.
"Can you give me an example?" he said.

"Sure. I think to quantify my goals means I should ask for a 5% salary increase instead of simply saying 'I want a raise', or I should say I trained fourteen employees last month, instead of saying 'I trained new hirers."

"Bingo," Bryan said excitedly. "It looks like you have a good understanding of quantification to me."

"Now the second trick"—he continued—"is the most important of all and it is one that most people overlook. I think the problem is that people have never been taught to do this and it's a real game changer. I guess people over-look it because it is so simple."

As Bryan paused for a moment to emphasize the significance of what he was about to say, Paige straightened up in her seat.

He went on, "At least five to eight months in advance you need to meet with your immediate supervisor, or whoever has the power to approve your raise or promotion, to discuss your goals as well as any necessary actions on your part to earn a raise or promotion. **This initial meeting with your boss is very important and it disappoints me that so many people overlook it.**"

"I have a performance review every year that is scheduled months in advance, often times falling on the same day every year. Why do I need to meet with my supervisor before my scheduled yearly performance review?" Paige inquired.

"How has meeting with your boss only on the day of your performance review worked out for you so far in your career?" Bryan uttered sarcastically.

Paige hung her head and grumbled, "Touché."

"Don't feel bad. **Millions of people make the same mistake every year.** Many employees erroneously think tenure is an automatic green light for raises and promotions, and others just assume their boss is paying close attention to them and keeping detailed records of work accomplishments by their employees. To further complicate matters, a lot of employees think their expectations are exactly the same as their boss' expectations. Most people never stop to ask their boss 'what do you expect from me?' It takes almost no time at all for an employee to ask this question in a private one-on-one meeting, yet millions of people every year never do. For example, before Ty left, what did he require of you each quarter in order for you to earn a raise or promotion?"

Dumbfounded, Paige sat quietly as she racked her brain to find an answer, but nothing came to mind. Finally, she reluctantly gave up and said, "I know this may sound silly since he has been my boss for the past six years, but I honestly don't know."

"You are not alone Paige. Believe me. I see this ALL the time. The biggest hindrance to most employees getting raises or promotions continues to be a lack of communication between employees and employers. You see, if employees and bosses would both grasp the fact that **NO ONE IS A MIND READER** then everyone would take the next step and respectfully ask for whatever it is that they want. Don't ever assume under any circumstance that another person is thinking the exact same thing or the same way as you. The proven, absolute best way to make certain that you are on the same page with someone is to simply ask them and, rest assured, their answer will clue you in to their perspective of the situation. I hate the guessing game and I hate not knowing where I stand with others. So, I make it a habit to open my mouth and ask people questions like 'Where do I stand with you?', 'What do you expect from me?' or, 'Can you help me reach my goal please?'"

Paige soaked in his advice and took notes. As quickly as the words left Bryan's lips, Paige's pen zoomed across the paper giving little concern to legibility.

Bryan paused, "Stop me at any time if you need clarification on anything."
"Oh, trust me I will. Please, keep going," she replied with excitement in her voice.

Bryan unbuttoned his sports coat, "The reason you should meet with your boss at least five months in advance of your performance review is so you both can write down the requirements that must be completed in order for you to achieve your goals. The purpose of the initial meeting with your boss is to get in the same book, in the same chapter, on the same page, and on the same line with each other. It is so easy for people to misunderstand and misinterpret each other without clear communication. The meeting with your supervisor will clear up all misunderstandings, which will make for a smoother path going forward."

"Sorry to interrupt, but what did you mean by requirements?" Paige asked.

"Oh no problem. Another word for requirements can be expectations, which will serve as a checklist for you and your boss to keep score of your progress. For example, requirements can address daily punctuality, workspace cleanliness, monthly sales quota, an increase or decrease of any of your job related metrics, decisiveness in decision making, added creativity, timeliness in responding to work emails, embracing a larger leadership role, personality adjustments, interpersonal conversational adjustments, attitude adjustments, intonation adjustments, continued education, or completion of education certifications. Oh, and any time you discuss requirements or expectations, do your best to quantify the requirements as much as possible so that when it comes time, everyone involved will be able to track your process objectively. Don't stress too much if some requirements and expectations can't be quantified, just quantify the ones that you can. That way at the end of the five month assessment period, there won't be any confusion or debate as to whether or not you qualify for the raise or promotion."

"Oh now I see," Paige said excitedly. "If I meet with my boss at least five months before my performance review then it is more likely that both my boss and I will have a clear understanding of what it will take for me to get a raise or a promotion. Also, my boss will be able to quickly research if the company has the money, resources, or assets that I requested during our initial meeting. If the company can't afford it, then my boss and I can renegotiate early in the process, instead of me getting blindsided with bad news on the day of my performance review. If the company does have the money or resources that I asked for, then my boss can begin picturing me in a leadership role. I read somewhere that 'success must first be visualized before it can be achieved.' Why didn't I think of that before? It makes so much sense and it's so simple. Now it all makes sense. Ty and I were never in the same chapter, much less on the same page. I never took the time to lay out my goals for him and I didn't ask him to list out the requirements for a raise or a promotion. I now see why raises and promotions have come so sparingly to me."

"Well said Paige!" Bryan proudly exclaimed.

Paige was happy to learn this new trick and wished she had thought to meet with her bosses to clarify expectations prior to her past performance reviews. Bryan had opened her mind to a new way of thinking and she could already see the many benefits of his suggestions. With four more meetings to go, Paige was excited to learn more ways of getting a raise or promotion. She could not wait for next week's meeting.

HELPFUL TIPS:

- Read the book *Whoever Makes the Most Mistakes Wins* by Richard Farson and Ralph Keyes.
- Embrace your differences and learn to accept the fact that you are not like everyone else.

SUMMARY NOTES:

1. Write down your goals.
2. Quantify your goals.
3. Meet with your supervisor at least 5 months in advance of your performance review to discuss your goals along with their requirements and expectations for you to earn a raise or promotion.

Chapter 4

Meetings on Meetings on Meetings

To effectively communicate,
we must realize that we are all different
in the way we perceive the world and
use this understanding as a guide to our communication with others.
—Tony Robbins

Criticism may not be agreeable, but it is necessary.
It fulfills the same function as pain in the human body.
It calls attention to an unhealthy state of things.
—Winston Churchill

The next week, Paige brought her lunch and ate in the conference room with the hope that Bryan would agree to start their meeting a little early. Her desire to learn more about acquiring raises and promotions had spiked. For the next three weeks, Wednesdays would be the highlight of her week. Tuesday nights were challenging however. She could barely sleep as she anxiously anticipated the sound of her phone's alarm clock.

As she sat in the conference room alone, her face brimmed with excitement. Nothing short of an unexpected natural disaster could wipe the smile from her face.

She had written down her goals and reviewed her notes from their first meeting. She wanted to impress Bryan. She greatly admired his patience and respected his ability to make the information relatable, practical, and easy to understand. Bryan, she thought, was an excellent mentor.

"I see that you brought your own supplies this time, and you even bought a leather folder—look at you go!" Bryan acclaimed as he closed the door to the conference room. He was pleased to see that Paige was taking his mentorship seriously.

"Well, if I don't put your advice into practice, what good is it going to do?" she gibed back. Bryan smiled in agreement.
"So, what's on the agenda for today?"

"Today we're going to discuss the importance of scheduling regular follow-up meetings with your superior," he affirmed.

Paige picked up her pen and prepared to take notes as Bryan continued.

"You need to meet with your boss once a month at the very least. If you both agree to meet more regularly, then that's fine. But meeting at least once a month is absolutely necessary."

"Why is that? Let's assume that I did what you recommended in the first meeting; shouldn't my boss and I collectively be on the same page? If so, why should we meet once a month until the date of my performance review?" Paige asked.

"The short answer is that people forget—more easily than they themselves might be willing to admit," Bryan answered.

"And the long answer?" Paige pressed.

Bryan eagerly took the bait. "Although you and your boss may now have a clear understanding of what it will take for you to achieve your goal, you need to schedule frequent meetings in order to keep your goals at the forefront of your boss's mind. If your goals change for whatever reason, make sure to tell your boss as soon as possible to keep them in the loop."

"In fact"—he continued—"quite a few scientific studies have been conducted over the years and scientists found that people forget things for two reasons. First, it is possible the memory has simply disappeared and it is no longer available. Secondly, sometimes the memory is still stored in the memory system but, for some reason, it cannot be retrieved. Memory tends to decay and gets worse as the time between learning and recall increases. So to increase the likelihood that your boss will remember your goals, you need to shorten the time-frame that you both discuss your goals. In essence, regularly scheduled follow-up meetings will make your boss much less likely to forget your goal, which in your case, is to get a raise or a promotion.[2]

"That makes perfect sense," Paige responded.

"I think so," Bryan acknowledged. "In fact, consistent follow-up meetings will also allow your boss to give you timely feedback on your progress. Although your boss laid out the expectations and requirements necessary for you to earn your raise or promotion in the first meeting, their feedback along the way is critical in order to let both of you know how you are doing. So in terms of priorities, **the initial meeting with your boss months before your performance review would be at the very top of the list. Then immediately followed by regular follow-up meetings to discuss your progress.**"

Paige interrupted, "Oh, so if my boss told me to dress more professionally, for example, then my boss will have the opportunity to assess the clothes I wear in-between our meetings. At our next meeting, they can tell me if the changes I made to my wardrobe meet their expectations. If however, my style does not meet their standards then they can tell me what I need to change. I can then use their feedback to make the necessary changes and try again."

"Bingo!" Bryan exclaimed. "But Paige, I don't think any boss in their right mind will have a problem with your professional attire. I mean, you always dress fabulously from what I can tell—albeit it has only been a few weeks of knowing you. But I have to applaud your style. You really have an eye for color coordination and accessorizing. I'm honestly impressed."

"Awww… thank you Bryan! You made my day. That compliment really means a lot!"

"Again, I'm impressed," Bryan said. "Your style is professional and you don't go over the top in any way."

"Thank you for your feedback." Paige brushed her shoulders off.

"This is an example of the power and importance of feedback," Bryan pointed out. "Feedback can be used to tell you what you're doing well and it can alert you to the things you might need to improve. Feedback is a critical cog in the loop of trying to get raises and promotions. It can be used to find out what your boss thinks about you. Feedback is also a great way to literally check-off any requirements that your boss has discussed with you. You can use this checklist of expectations to gauge how much further you have to go to reach your goal."

Bryan spent twenty minutes discussing the benefits of scheduling follow-up meetings. The more information he dished out, the more Paige's curiosity grew. Bryan utilized an assortment of examples to show that asking for feedback would most likely reiterate to her boss that she was serious about attaining her goal.

He also spent a great detail of time explaining that interpersonal communication is littered with misunderstandings. For example, he explained to Paige that Person A's understanding of Person B's message could be totally different from the message Person B tried to convey. He then showed Paige how feedback can clear up misunderstandings for all parties involved.

"Can you give me some tips on how I should receive feedback since I'll be sitting in at least a dozen follow-up meetings every year?" Paige asked.

"Sure," Bryan said with delight. "There are three areas that you should focus on improving."

"Lay em' on me," Paige responded.

"First, you want to exhibit a warm, welcoming demeanor to show your boss that you sincerely want their feedback. You will do yourself no favors if you come across as confrontational, argumentative, tired, uninterested, or bored. Along those same lines, don't sulk, frown, or fidget around in your seat.

To avoid appearing aloof, you should sit up straight and maintain a pleasant facial expression throughout the entirety of your meetings. So many people don't understand how important it is to smile when someone else is talking. I mean, even a faint smile that doesn't show any teeth is better than a person sitting there with a bland, stoic look on their face. It bothers me so much when I talk to someone and they do not smile. Come on now, how hard is it to pull your dimples back and smile?" Bryan replied.

A short laugh escaped Paige's lips as her pen skated across the paper capturing Bryan's insightful pointers.

"Second"—Bryan kept going—"look your boss in the eyes when they are speaking. After your boss has finished making their point, repeat what they said in your own words just to make certain you understand what they said. After your boss confirms that you understood the information exactly how it was intended, then you can quickly jot down a few notes."

"Third, you should focus the conversations on what your boss thinks you are doing well and the areas that they think you can improve. Your boss's feedback is paramount and since they are the final decision makers to determine whether you get a raise or not, you need to let them do the talking. Don't interrupt your boss midsentence even if it's to agree with them. Also, you are not there to ramble on about your day, grievances, or how you think you are doing.

If they ask for your perspective, then quickly answer their question, but do your best to not hog the conversation. It's in your best interest to let your boss do the talking. If, however, your boss isn't much of a talker, then I suggest you ask them some open-ended questions to get them to talk about your work performance. You can also ask them for feedback in regards to each of the requirements and expectations discussed in the first meeting. Just do your best to get your boss to give you feedback, make eye contact, repeat back what they said, and take notes," Bryan concluded.

"What if I have suggestions that can improve, expedite, or make something more efficient?" Paige chimed in.

"There is nothing wrong with presenting innovative ideas to your boss in your follow-up meetings. Just make sure to first give your boss the opportunity to speak candidly and uninterrupted about your job performance. As a matter of fact, your boss's perspectives of your job performance should take up 2/3 of the meeting. The last 1/3 of the meeting is where you can respectfully offer your input to improve X, Y, or Z," Bryan answered.

"If I do have grievances about someone in the office, how do I tell my boss without sounding like a tattle tell?" she responded.

"Hahaha. Write an anonymous note and slide it under your boss's door," Bryan joked. "I'm just kidding—don't ever do that.

First off, you should try to resolve the conflict with your adversary one-on-one. If that doesn't work then find an objective mediator to facilitate talks between you two. If all else fails, general policy is to notify HR and ask for their advice on how to remedy the situation. In each of these sit-downs, at the onset say something positive about the person you have the grievance with. Then briefly explain how their actions affected you and describe how those actions made you feel. Next, state the actions that you took to try to rectify the problem and close with something positive about finding a solution to the problem."

"That's perfect! Thanks Bryan," Paige asserted. "Sorry if my questions are silly."

"Your questions are not silly at all," Bryan reassured her.

"So you said I should never interrupt my boss when they are speaking, but what if I don't agree with the feedback given to me? What if what my boss is saying is outright wrong? I don't want to appear confrontational or argumentative, but I don't want misinformation to go uncorrected. How do I handle those situations?" Paige asked.

"Fantastic question!" Bryan exclaimed. "So before you attempt to explain yourself and clarify something your boss said, in your mind, you need to first weigh the necessity of adding your two cents.

99% of the time when your boss gives you feedback, the correct and only answer should be 'thank you'. Nothing more nothing less. Don't try to justify your actions or explain your thought process. Just say 'thank you' then take notes if applicable. For example, if your boss said you need to start coming in to work on time every day. Just say 'thank you', make a note of it, and let that be the end of that discussion. There's zero need to explain your prior tardiness. Just say 'thank you' and get to work on time from that moment on."[3]

"On the few occasions when you must address and correct your boss's analysis, be confident in knowing that it is okay to standup for yourself—respectfully of course," Bryan continued. "For major discrepancies say, 'thank you for your honest feedback. I would like to respectfully address X, Y, and Z.' Then **succinctly** give your understanding of the situation by stating your point of view without telling the entire background or the detailed version of the story. Keep your story short. Think cliff notes version kind of short. Introduce the people involved, give a brief synopsis of the situation, tell your boss the actions that you specifically made, then state how the situation was rectified. If your boss wants clarification on any specific part of the story then they will ask for you to go into greater detail—otherwise keep it short."

"What sort of discrepancies would fall under the 1% that I am permitted to offer clarification?" Paige inquired.

"Big things such as a perceived failure to meet deadlines, fiscal mismanagement, budgeting, explicit delineation of someone's employment expectations/job description/role, lost sales, severed relationships, or miscommunications that lead to any of the aforementioned areas fall under that 1%. Otherwise the correct answer is to say 'thank you' and end discourse on the matter," Bryan stated.

"You have really given me so much to think about. In a good way of course," Paige said appreciatively.

"Next week I will teach you how to impress your boss at your follow-up meetings and how you can prove to them that you deserve a raise," Bryan teased.

"I can't wait," replied Paige.

HELPFUL TIPS:

- Actively seek out feedback from your boss, co-workers, friends, family, and acquaintances. Feedback is the life-blood to improvement and self-growth.
- Be proactive and ask for what you want.

SUMMARY NOTES:

1. Schedule regular follow-up meetings with your boss.
2. Display a warm, welcoming, non-confrontational demeanor when your boss gives you feedback.
3. Sit up straight and smile gently in every meeting.
4. Make eye contact with your boss, repeat what they said in your own words, and then quickly take notes if applicable.
5. Conversations with your boss should center on what your boss thinks you are doing well and the areas that they think you can improve.
6. Your boss's perspectives of your job performance should take up 2/3 of the meeting.
7. The last 1/3 of the meeting is where you can humbly and respectfully offer your inputs and suggestions.
8. 99% of the time when your boss gives you feedback, the correct and only answer should be 'thank you'. Nothing more nothing less.
9. Don't try to justify your actions or explain your thought process. Just say 'thank you' then take notes if applicable.
10. 1% of the time when you need to clarify misunderstandings, know that it's okay to stand up for yourself.

11. To rectify conflicts with co-workers, start by saying something positive about the person, then briefly explain how their actions made you feel, next, state the actions that you took to rectify the problem, and close with something positive about the person.

Chapter 5

See What I've Done

Don't let anyone tell your story. Pick up a pen and write your own.
—Majid Kazmi

I am only one, but I am one.
I cannot do everything, bud I can do something.
And because I cannot do everything,
I will not refuse to do the something that I can do.
—Edward Everett Hale

As Paige made her way to the conference room the following Wednesday, Kerry—her favorite person and closest confidant in the office—tapped her on the shoulder and showered her with compliments about her outfit.

"That is just the cutest purple scarf. And those shoes. I love D'Orsay Flats. Where did you get those shoes? They must have cost a fortune." Kerry blazoned.

The two friends chatted for a while and promised to grab brunch soon to catchup on all the happenings in each other's life.

As Paige walked into the conference room, she was shocked to see that Bryan was eagerly awaiting their chat. She wanted to be the first to arrive but was more than happy to start their meeting a few minutes early.

They exchanged pleasantries before Bryan jumped right into the topic for the day.

"Over the last two meetings, we discussed the importance of the initial meeting with your boss along with the benefits of receiving honest feedback about your job performance through consistent follow-up meetings. Today, I will teach you what items you should take with you to all of your meetings," Bryan announced.

Paige held up her black leather folder in her left hand and notepad in her right hand. "Check and check," she said, grinning.

"That's a great start," Bryan acknowledged. "But do you know what to put inside that folder?"

"Aside from my notepad, a few pens, and some of my business cards, I actually have no idea," she conceded.

"You mastered the note taking part, but you are not relegated to take notes on an actual paper notepad if you don't want. If it's easier for you, feel free to use your laptop, an app on your cell-phone, a tablet, notecards, or even sticky notes to jot down notes from the meetings," he clarified. "It makes little sense to write down notes on a paper notepad if your plan is to later transfer the information to the cloud for instance, so why not use the device that's easiest for you to be more time efficient?"

"I concur," Paige admitted.

Bryan took a sip of water from his water bottle, "Most people mistakenly wait till their yearly performance reviews to present all of their proof that they deserve a raise to their boss. But that's not what you're going to do, right Paige?"

"Of course not," she answered back. "Tell me again, why am I not going to wait till my yearly performance review to show my boss that I deserve a raise?"

"You mean aside from the fact that you are smarter than most people?" Bryan jested.

"Yep. Aside from that obvious fact," she acquiesced.

"Because you are going to take full advantage of all of the follow-up meetings with your boss leading up to your final performance review to prove you deserve a raise or promotion. Instead of dumping all of your proof on their desk the day of your performance review, you are going to submit quantifiable proof of your achievements to your boss at every meeting. Your boss will know ahead of time that you are kicking butt and taking names, and they will reward you with a raise because they will see months in advance that you deserve one."

"How am I going to do that again? I mean, how am I going to show them that I deserve a raise or a promotion?" she implored as she tried to make sense of what he was saying.

"You remember that 2/3 of your follow-up meetings with your boss should center on a list of things you are doing well and the areas that they think you can improve?" Bryan asked rhetorically. "You will use the last 1/3 of each meeting to give them written proof of how you addressed and corrected the areas that they suggested you needed to work on."

"What do you mean by 'written proof'?" she coaxed, using air quotes.

"For example, let's say that your boss comments on your consistent tardiness. You should keep a digital or written record of the times that you clocked in to work during the weeks that lead up to your next feedback meeting. Every morning when you arrive, you should write down the date, day of the week, and the time that you arrived to work. Then you will put that record inside your leather folder and be sure to give it to your boss as evidence that you addressed your tardiness issue and endeavored to fix the problem," Bryan explained.

"Aha, that makes sense," Paige acknowledged.

"In addition to keeping track of the improvements you were asked to make, you should track the things your boss mentioned that you did well. You want to show your boss that you will work hard to improve the areas they suggested need improvement but, at the same time, you will continue to do the things that they think you do well," Bryan went on. "From this moment on, I want you to keep track of each of your work accomplishments."

"Sounds easy enough," she countered. "But what do you mean by work accomplishments?"

"Work accomplishments can pertain to the metrics related to your position. For example, if you had a quota for the number of calls you had to make a day, then every time you exceed your call quota you should write down the date and the number of calls you made above your quota," he responded. "This can apply to exceeding your sales goals, client acquisitions, big deals you closed, times you helped employees overcome work hurdles, certifications or training programs that you completed, every project you completed on time or ahead of schedule, the number of new employees that you trained, tasks that you completed that are not a part of your job description, excess work that you put into projects, the instances you go above and beyond for your clients or customers, the times that you stepped in to prevent the escalation of work problems, the times you successfully resolved conflict, any novel ideas that you implemented that worked, any time you save the company money or increase workplace efficiency, lists of employees that you mentored, etc."

"So every time one of my customers fills out a comment card or email to say they are pleased with me, I should make a note of the positive feedback on my tablet and present it to my boss at the follow-up meetings?" asked Paige.

"Absolutely," answered Bryan. "Take the time to write down your work accomplishments, awards received, and any positive feedback that you received from others during the weeks in-between your feedback meetings. When you present the written proof of your achievements to your boss, ask them if they would like to keep a copy of your accomplishments and proceed accordingly."

"I'm thinking ahead and that seems like a lot of notes or paperwork that I'll accumulate. Am I supposed to hold on to all of that stuff for a few months?" Paige checked.

Bryan chuckled at her bewilderment, "Your notes should not be written in complete sentences. Instead, they should be bullet points that are short and straight to the point. Moreover, you should periodically summarize your list of accomplishments with the company you currently work for every six months, at the one year mark, the five year mark, the ten year mark, and so on."

Bryan went on to present a micro and a macro overview for recording work accomplishments. For the micro view, he used an example of Paige meeting with her boss every two weeks for six months. Every two weeks in-between follow-up meetings, she was responsible for notating her work accomplishments along with specific examples of improvements she made regarding the areas her boss suggested she needed to improve. If her boss suggested new areas for her to work on, she should write down the new tasks to tackle, track her progress, and present written proof that she addressed her deficiencies at their next meeting. This process would continue for six months and she should bring six months' worth of her accomplishments to her final review.

Next, Bryan took the time to explain the macro view of recording her achievements. He told her that every year she should summarize and narrow down her list of accomplishments for the entire year to a one page summary.

At the five year mark, he explained that she should have five one page summaries: one for each year that she tracked her accomplishments. He insisted, however, that after the fifth year, she should condense those summaries into one concise page of accomplishments.

At the ten year mark, Bryan suggested that Paige should again compress her list of accomplishments to one page. He wanted her to repeat this process every year if she was at the same company or even if she changed jobs.

When Bryan finished, Paige asked, "Is the summary of my accomplishments the same thing as my resume?"

"No. Your resume and your accomplishments should be viewed as two separate documents," Bryan responded. "You should have multiple versions of your resume that reflect the position that you are applying for. For instance, if you were applying for a job in sales, then your resume should be littered with phrases like 'sold', 'exceeded quota', 'sold $5,000,000 of merchandise each quarter', 'sales manager', etc. The same goes if you are applying for an accounting or marketing position. Your resume should be filled with the buzz words of the position for which you are applying."

"Your accomplishments on the other hand"—he continued—"might be too extensive to fit on your one to two page resume. Think about it. You should have six months worth of accomplishments that could range from uplifting customer comments to arriving at work on time. There's just no way to fit all of that information on your resume and—quite frankly—some of it might look outright awkward there. You can however give interviewers both your resume and your one page list of accomplishments to distinguish yourself and to give them a glimpse of your prior achievements. I have interviewed thousands of people over the years and I can tell you that employers and interviewers are always looking for reasons to throw your resume in the trash, but they are also looking for exceptional people who can differentiate themselves from the herd."

Paige vigorously took notes as she gently smiled in agreement. At the end of his lengthy speech, Paige added, "So, if I kept succinct records of my accomplishments, it would not only be great for my current boss to assess my worth in the company, but it could be useful if new management took over. The new manager will be able to get a quick snap shot of my past success at the company, my work ethic, attention to detail, my willingness to accept honest feedback, and my desire to excel at this company."

"I couldn't have said it better myself," Bryan nodded, as he gave his seal of approval.

In the last few minutes of their meeting, Bryan discussed the option for Paige to schedule one or two meetings with her immediate boss's boss. But he cautioned her though, that she should not schedule a meeting with her boss's boss before her second follow-up meeting with her immediate superior in order to prevent appearing as though she was trying to go over his head. Bryan then recommended that Paige introduce herself to her boss's boss and spend the first few minutes learning about their past, accomplishments to date, and the circumstances that brought them to their current position. After she learned a little bit about their successes, he told her to succinctly state her goals and briefly give a positive overview of her meetings with her immediate boss.

Bryan then listed a few benefits of introducing yourself to your boss's boss:

- The new connection could become a personal friend or confidant
- The introduction could open doors to unforeseen career opportunities that might help you climb the corporate ladder
- Any advice or recommendations given could spur character development and add to your internal wealth

"Next time we meet"—Bryan hinted—"we'll discuss how you can win over your co-workers and your boss with kindness during your evaluation period."

As they concluded their meeting, Paige's mind swarmed with her accomplishments over the last eight years at the company. She could not wait to write them all down.

HELPFUL TIPS:

- Take notes in a form that is easy and efficient for you, including handwritten or digital format.

SUMMARY NOTES:

1. Keep written records of any improvements that you were asked to make.
2. Keep written records of the things your boss told you that you did well and that you continued to do.
3. Keep written records of your accomplishments during the months leading up to your performance review.
4. Every year, condense your list of accomplishments for the entire year to a one page summary.
5. Every five years, condense your five one page summaries to a single page.
6. Every ten years, compact your list of achievements to one page.
7. Your resume and your list of work accomplishments are not the same thing.
8. Schedule a meeting with your boss's boss after your second follow-up meeting with your immediate supervisor.

Chapter 6

High Five for Him, High Five for Her, Everybody Gets a High Five

> Be kind whenever possible. It is always possible.
> —Tenzin Gyatso

> If someone were to pay you ten cents
> for every kind word you said about people and
> collect five cents for every unkind word,
> would you be rich or poor?
> —Jacob M. Braude

The following week, both Paige and Bryan tried to beat the other to the conference room but, instead, arrived at the same time. Bryan held the door open as her pale gold high heels click-clacked across the floor.

"Are those Michael Kors?" Bryan asked.

"They sure are," Paige answered. "And I love your 'Big Knot' tie. The faint grey in your tie really stands out with your light grey suit. But the orange and purple plaid in your tie contrasts beautifully with your whole ensemble. I love it!"

As they sat down, Bryan opened his leather folder and removed his stapled checklist. While he flipped to the second page, Paige powered on her tablet to take notes.

"No pen and paper today?" Bryan gibed.

"Haha. Since my list of goals and pretty much everything else is in my email, I figured this would save me some time. Plus, my tablet will make it much easier for me to share your tips with my friends," she smirked.

"Very good," Bryan commended. "Well today, you are going to learn how you should carry yourself during the evaluation period for your raise or promotion. As always, feel free to pepper me with questions if something I say needs clarifying."

"Will do," Paige responded.

Bryan skimmed over the notion that Paige should not voice her complaints about co-workers to fellow co-workers. If she had a legitimate complaint with a person, he told her to respectfully confront that person or find a mediator to facilitate a solution, most likely via HR. Gossip was a huge no-no from his perspective.

He went on to say that gossipers are not looked upon favorably by their co-workers. The irony, he pointed out, was that most people simply avoid chatting with a gossip whenever possible rather than confronting the rabble-rouser about their gossip issue.

He then touched on the subject of removing negativity from her vocabulary to instead focus on phrasing her statements with positivity.

"I don't understand," she said. "How do I discard negative statements and replace them with positive ones? Can you give me an example?"

"Sure," Bryan obliged. "Let's say you received a raise and..."

"Heck yeah!" Paige cheered as she pumped her fist in the air. "Money-money-money-MONEY!" she sang.

Bryan chuckled then continued, "One day while chitchatting around the watercooler, the topic of Chance's tardiness came up. Everyone in the group joked about the fact that Chance can't seem to get anywhere or complete any task on time. Instead of following the proverbial herd, you can say something like 'I appreciate it when Chance does show up on time.' Now, the rest of the group might jump on that opening to say something like, 'That's like what, once or twice a year?' But as you can see in my example, you can find something positive to say about your co-workers when everyone else is speaking negatively about them. Your comment will be positive, and you contribution to the conversation won't be a lie."

Bryan even mentioned a few scientific studies that showed negativity, complaining, and stress can all have an adverse effect on the human body. In one such study, he pointed out, when your brain is firing off synapses of anger, you weaken your immune system by raising your blood pressure, which can increase your risk for heart disease, obesity, and diabetes.[4]

Bryan also referenced Mayo Clinic's tips and strategies on how people can first identify negative thinking in order to focus on positive thinking.[5]

"People really do not enjoy being around Debbie Downers for long periods of time," Bryan commented as he causally changed the subject.

"Moving on to sharing credit," he continued. "You need to publicly recognize your co-workers when they submit a good idea, suggest a helpful solution to a problem, go above and beyond, or any time they do something praise worthy. You don't have to wait until you are the boss or a manager to give out praise. Don't wait *'for the right moment'* to tell someone 'thank you' or 'job well done'. In fact, you should never delay showing appreciation in the moment, with the idea that you will say 'thank you' through some grand gesture later. Take a quick second to say, 'good job' publicly as quickly as possible. After your immediate gesture of recognition, you can offer further tribute at a later time in a different way if you think it would be appreciated or helpful. Despite the possibility of repeated credit, do not neglect the initial display of gratitude."

"Are you saying I should praise every little thing someone does all day long, because honestly, I don't want to seem fake?" Paige hesitantly inquired.

"Oh no. For example, don't go around the office publically congratulating Melissa for holding her pen just right, or applauding Brittany for not falling out of her swivel chair this week… although, that would be pretty funny," Bryan joked. "In all seriousness though, freely and publicly salute your co-workers when they exceed expectations or surpass their work metrics."

"I guess along the same lines"—Paige added—"I should never applaud someone privately for a good idea but, later publicly steal their praise by implying that I was the one who came up with the idea or solution."

"Precisely," Bryan agreed. "Your boss is probably paying close attention to how you treat everyone you interact with while you're on the clock, so it's in your best interest to speak and act with class. You can portray a demeanor of elegance by being humble, showing respect, and owning up to your personal job mistakes. Your boss isn't the only one who is assessing your character and your actions. Your co-workers are also keeping a watchful eye on how you treat your fellow co-workers and believe me, they won't forget so easily when you wrong them."

"That's so true," Paige agreed. "I can still think of a few instances when my co-workers or even Ty did something that rubbed me the wrong way. From now on, I promise I will make a conscious effort to publicly praise my co-workers. That way, when I get a raise or promotion my co-workers will celebrate with me and think it was well deserved."

"Bryan, what about bringing donuts or lunch to the office? Isn't that a good way to win my co-workers over?"

"I think bringing breakfast, lunch, or some kind of snack is a great way to endear your co-workers and boss to you," he remarked. "If you choose to bring food to the office, however, just make sure there's plenty for everyone and don't do it too often. Once or twice a month should be fine, but keep in mind it can quickly become quite expensive. Plus, you don't want to do it too often because your co-workers may come to expect it or worse—they might think you are brown-nosing. You want others to perceive your gesture to be genuine so be sure to also mix up the days that you bring food. To answer your question, I think you should bring food for the office at least twice during your evaluation period, but try to bring something healthy if you can. Donuts, although they are delicious, aren't particularly good for you."

In the last portion of their meeting, Paige frantically typed as Bryan cleared up the notion that the opinions of her co-workers were just as important as those of her boss. He also highlighted the many benefits of going the extra mile on every project or task she undertook.

Paige curiously wondered what they would discuss in their last scheduled meeting but, this time, Bryan offered no hints.

HELPFUL TIPS:

- Make time to send out handwritten thank you notes and letters.

SUMMARY NOTES:

1. Do not voice your complaints to fellow co-workers.
2. Be positive and remove negativity from your speech.
3. Praise your co-workers' achievements publicly and immediately.
4. Do not claim your co-worker's ideas as your own.
5. Your boss and co-workers are assessing daily your actions so act and speak with class.
6. Be humble, show respect to everyone, and own up to your mistakes.
7. Bring healthy food for your office at least twice during your evaluation period.
8. Arrive to work early every day.
9. Go the extra mile on all projects and assignments.

Chapter 7

Oh Grandpa Bill

Words are singularly the most powerful force available to humanity.
We can choose to use this force constructively with
words of encouragement, or destructively using words of despair.
Words have energy and power with the ability to help, to heal,
to hinder, to hurt, to harm, to humiliate and to humble.

—Yehuda Berg

Over the weekend Paige drove to see her favorite person in the world—her Grandpa Bill. She loved listening to him play his guitar, sipping his homemade moonshine, and the fuzziness of his burly beard scratching her face every time he pulled her in tight for hugs and kisses. Most of all she enjoyed his unpredictable humor. Some people found Grandpa Bill's jokes offensive but, to her, he was a hoot.

"Why didn't you call to let me know you were stopping by child?" Grandpa Bill fussed.

"Umm, I did call and told you just yesterday that I was coming over today silly," Paige corrected.

"Well, it must be all these dang pills the doctor got me taking. It's a-messing with my memory you see." Grandpa Bill responded petulantly.

"You know, I keep crossing my fingers that one of these days you will admit when you're wrong," Paige replied.

Grandpa Bill grunted and held the screen door open for Paige while she got her raspberry handbag and cyan sweater from the trunk of her car.

As they walked to the kitchen, the muted television grabbed her attention. Tom and Jerry filled up every bit of the sixty-five inch flat screen. A warm smile appeared on her face as she remembered childhood summers passing the time curled up in Grandpa Bill's lap enjoying cartoon after cartoon. She made her way to the refrigerator and poured herself a glass of juice.

"What's all this I hear about you getting a promotion?" Grandpa Bill plopped down in his worn-out brown leather recliner.

"No Grandpa. They haven't given me the promotion yet, but an intern manager is teaching me a few tricks to help me get promotions more regularly in the future," Paige answered as she sipped her drink.

"If you ask me, all of them are darn fools if they don't give my baby a raise. Fools I tell you. FOOLS!" he emphasized, as he sat up in his recliner, shaking his finger pointedly at Paige.

She cracked a smile at his implicit compliment as she made her way over to the sectional next to his recliner.

"How much they paying you over there anyways? Oh it doesn't matter. I told you once and I'll tell it to you again. Why don't you come work for me and I'll pay you a nickel a day Honey Bear?" Grandpa Bill insisted.

Apple juice squirted from Paige's nose and collected on the coffee table in front of her. She could not hold in her laughter. Her cheeks flushed with warmth, her hands slapping at her knees. She could listen to him talk for hours. To her, Grandpa Bill's presence equaled non-stop laughter.

"Anyways, my coach or teacher—Bryan is his name—has taught me a lot so far and I can't wait to use some of his techniques," she said as she brushed off the apple juice from her white blouse and gathered herself.

"What's this schmuck teaching you that I haven't taught you?" Grandpa Bill challenged. "Has he taught you how to corral the heck outta some goats? Or how to get chickens to mate using a secret dance with pompoms? Or how to make a salty quiche?"

"No grandpa. He hasn't taught me any of those things but, you never know, since we have one more meeting to go," Paige snickered.

"Well then. If he ain't teaching you how to do some corralling real proper, then he ain't teaching ya nothing if you ask me," Grandpa Bill squawked.

"So far Bryan told me I need to set up an initial meeting with my boss to tell them that I would like a raise in five months or so. Next, he showed me the importance of scheduling consistent follow-up meetings to show my boss my work achievements, asking for feedback, and providing proof that I improved in the areas they said I needed to work on…" Paige answered.

"Oh that all sounds like hocus pocus," he interrupted.

"Grandpa, it's not hocus pocus. Bryan gave me some really good information that I had never thought of. For instance, I had no idea that I should praise someone publicly as quickly as possible or how to replace negative speech with positivity," Paige continued.

"The only thing you need to know about getting a raise is that your boss expects you to negotiate with them. They want you to counter their offer and play the game. For example, if you want a 12% raise but your boss counters with a measly 8%, don't just accept it. You need to tell that good for nothing potato head that 8% is good but you was thinking more like 12% but you are willing to compromise at 10%. Everybody knows all your bosses are gonna low ball you, but when they do, I want you to take out a pair of vice grips from your purse and set it on the table directly in front of them and don't say another word. I tell you what, that trick there worked like a charm when your grandmother's father had a little chat with me about marrying your grandmother and it sure did work for me back in that War of 1980." Grandpa Bill argued.

"Wait a sec. What war are you talking about grandpa?" Paige uttered.

"The Cold War my child. I wasn't gonna let those—I can't even say their name—win so I rounded up a few of the boys and we rode our tractors over yonder to the nearest town and vice-gripped anyone who didn't look American! You young punks got me and my tractor buddies to thank for ending that war."

"Oh my word. Grandpa!" Paige said dumbfounded as she was caught off guard.

"Let me tell you something else. Don't be afraid to negotiate for a pay raise you hear. Your boss expects you to negotiate…" he echoed.

"Grandpa, you already said that," Paige patted his knee.

"I sure did didn't I. Well it's the truth and you needed to hear it twice," he groaned. "You need to do your research before you ask for a raise also. Use that there computer thing-a-ma-giggy to find out what other people in your field are making. I still for the life of me don't understand that box. Anyways, them companies these days go around cheating young, pretty girls like you by not paying them what they pay them male folk. No ma'am. Not my Honey Bear. My baby is gonna do her homework and know what she is worth. Ain't that right?"

"You're sure right Grandpa. I will make sure to do my research on that box thing-a-ma-giggy to find out what my peers are making to make sure my company doesn't cheat me out of any nickels," Paige parroted.

"And another thing…" Grandpa cut in. "Don't walk into your meeting with the boss looking all desperate and pitiful like Old Man Darren's three legged dog. I want you to jerk your shoulders back, standup straight, and put some bass in your voice when you ask for that raise. You hear me? I don't want you whispering, fidgeting with your hands, mumbling, or acting all nervous in there. I want you to be decisive and look confident even if you're shaking like a three-legged mutt on the inside. You hear me Child?"

"I hear you loud and clear Grandpa."

"Before I forget, don't give that company no ultimatum either unless you actually have a second job lined up and in the bag. The last thing you want is to tell that company 'I want a raise or else I'm quitting' and have them spit shine their boot before swift kicking your butt outta there just like your cousin Tommy. It's been twelve years and you know that boy still ain't found him no job yet? What a shame," Grandpa Bill scoffed.

They talked for a few hours as time skated by. These were the moments Paige lived for; unfettered conversations with her grandfather. He rarely said it but he enjoyed her company a lot. The passing of his wife left a void in his world, but Paige's phone calls and visits made every day worth living.

Paige broke the brief silence, "Grandpa, I'm thinking about getting Bryan a gift as my way of saying 'thank you' for all his help."

Grandpa Bill answered, "This Bryan guy, he better not be trying no foolishness with you. You hear me? I'll march right on up to that office of his and serve him up a good ole fashion whooping with a side of round-house kicks. Them boys these days needs to watch their motions. You hear me? They need to watch their motions."

Paige was thoroughly amused at the thought of her grandfather attempting a round-house kick much less landing one on Bryan.

"No grandpa. He's not like that at all. He's a perfect gentleman. I just want to get him something thoughtful that's not pretentious. Should I get him a tie?" she implored.

"He sounds like a nancy and probably already have a ton of ties. Why don't you get him a pocket protector? Or a samurai sword? You can't have enough protection these days," Grandpa Bill razzed.

Paige let him ramble for a while as her mind wandered. She pictured an assortment of gift items for her mentor. That's it she thought—a watch would be the perfect gift. Bryan was a sharp dresser and would appreciate the addition of a hand watch to his chic wardrobe collection.

As Paige and her grandfather exchanged goodbyes, hugs, and kisses, her excitement grew at the thought of giving Bryan a watch at their final meeting.

HELPFUL TIPS:

- Always pause for 10 seconds to gather your thoughts before you speak.
- Take some time to call up and visit the older folks in your life.
- Make time for family and friends. Life can get busy but people are the most important things in this world.

SUMMARY NOTES:

1. Most bosses expect their employees to negotiate their pay raise.
2. Research the salaries of peers in your field before negotiating a raise.
3. Square your shoulders and sit-up straight in order to look confident when you ask for a raise.
4. Do not give ultimatums! When negotiating compensation packages during the interview or asking for a raise after you have been hired, use phrases that leave room for negotiation such as "What do you think about that?", "Would that amount be possible?" or, "How do you feel about that?".
5. Men and women, watch your motions and maintain professional behavior in the workplace.

Chapter 8
Show Me the Money!

When you want something this badly, you don't just give up.
You fight and fight until you absolutely can't fight anymore.
—Gail McHugh

Money and salary is not a particularly good motivator
in the long term.
—Matt Mullenweg

With her gift sharply wrapped and bedecked with a bow, Paige skipped lunch to work on her current project in the conference room, happy to arrive before Bryan.

Paige could not control her excitement. She anticipated Bryan's look of surprise when he opened her heartfelt gift. Her face radiated with joy as her smile spread across rosy cheeks.

She typed absentmindedly, doing her best to focus on her work but having little success. As the time drew closer to the start of their meeting, questions filled her mind while the debate within her intensified. Should she give Bryan the present at the beginning or at the end of their meeting? Was this an appropriate gift for someone she had only known for six weeks? Would he accept her token of appreciation? What would she do with the watch if he turned it down? Would Grandpa Bill wear this kind of watch?

She heard the door crack open. *It's game time* she thought.

"A few of us are going to grab drinks after work. Would you like to join? Let me rephrase. Peter Vo might be going and if he does, I NEED you to be there. Please?" Richard pleaded.

"Sure, I'll tag along," she said amicably, hoping Richard would scurry along before Bryan arrived.

Before the door settled comfortably back to a close, she heard a voice that had become rather familiar.

"Hey Paige," Bryan exclaimed. "How are you doing today?"

Too excited to process or even answer his question, she slid her present across the table as Bryan made his way to his seat.

"What's this?" He asked.
"Oh it's nothing. Well, it's a little something to say 'thank you' for taking the time to teach me how to get a raise," Paige murmured as her face turned beat red.

Bryan gently removed the sky-blue bow and proceeded to patiently unwrap the present, careful not to tear the paper.

As he caught a glimpse of the watch, his face lit up with appreciation.

"Thank you so much! This is awesome!" Bryan blurted out. "You know you didn't have to get me anything right?"

"Of course I didn't have to but I wanted to. This is the least I can do to show my appreciation," Paige admitted.

Bryan jumped up from his seat and came around the table to give Paige a heartfelt hug. The two spent a few minutes pointing out some of the watch's features that impressed them both. Bryan continued to praise her for such a thoughtful gift and Paige felt more at ease with her purchase decision.

As Bryan transitioned to the topic of the day, he opened his leather folder and again removed the stapled papers he seemed to always carry.

"Today, we're going to discuss some of the things you can ask for during your yearly performance reviews."

"Oh that's easy. I'm going to ask for more money and a promotion," Paige said matter-of-factly.

"Yes, money and promotions are two things that you can ask for, but there are others to think about as well," Bryan countered. "For starters, you need to understand that you should ask for something every year. It doesn't really matter what you ask for, but you should ask for something every year no matter what company you work for."

"Like What? Other than money and promotions, what else would the company give me in exchange for my hard work, creativity, and dedication?" Paige challenged.

"Here's another way to look at it. Do you have family members and friends that you would like to spend more time with?" Bryan pressed.

Her Grandpa Bill and Kerry quickly came to mind. "I sure do," she replied, still not quite catching on to what Bryan meant.

"You can ask your boss to increase the number of days you are allowed to work remotely. So, instead of coming into the office five or six days a week, you can work from home, a local coffee shop, or from another city perhaps, two or three days out of the week," Bryan explained. "That would give you the opportunity to stay with your Grandpa Bill throughout the week, or you and Kerry could schedule brunch, lunch, or dinner dates more regularly if you were not tied down to the office."

Bryan could see the light bulb come on for Paige. She paused her notetaking and stared inquisitively at Bryan as she contemplated the many benefits of having the freedom to work remotely.

"You can also ask for more vacation days or even a paid vacation courtesy of your company," Bryan continued. "Who wouldn't want to stay an extra day or two on the lovely island of Grenada? Better yet, who wouldn't want an all-expense paid vacation to Hawaii? Do you travel outside of the country?" he asked.

The two spoke briefly about their past travel escapades, pointing out hidden gems within the places they both ventured. They also discussed cities they both had on wish lists that they hoped to visit one day.

"Would it be inappropriate of me to ask for a business expense account?" Paige probed.

"Not at all," Bryan reassured her. "You can ask for a general business expense account to use at your own discretion, or you can ask for a meal expense account to entertain clients. You can also ask for a company phone, a company computer, a company car, or reimbursement for work related expenses if it seems appropriate to you."

"Okay, okay. What about a clothing expense account?" Paige teased, hoping, but doubting, the answer would be yes.

"Haha. You can always ask for it and see what your boss says," Bryan bantered back. "From my experience, it never hurts to ask. The worst they can say is no, and probably fire you on the spot. Just kidding," he laughed. "In all seriousness, don't be afraid to ask for the things that you value or you're interested in. However, make sure to ask for things that are related in some way to your job description and tasks. Don't try to milk the company for unnecessary perks that aren't appropriate. Now keep in mind that everyone is different so you will find many people who are motivated by things other than money or a bigger office. For example, spending time with family or young children might be more important to some folks. You need to write down the things that would motivate you to work harder at your company and ask your boss for those things in your initial meeting when you discuss the expectations for you to get a raise or promotion; but instead of asking for money, you will request other things that motivate you."

"Back to money for a second," she backtracked, "If I ask for more money, how much should I ask for? What's a reasonable amount from your experience?"

"To answer your question, you can ask for a 1%—20% raise. If you want to leave room for negotiation you can ask for a percent slightly higher than what you want. Ask for anything higher than 20% though, and your boss may give you a crazy look coupled with a resounding 'NO'. Along the lines of asking for more money, you can also ask your boss to increase the amount that your company will match towards your 401k. My preferred method is to ask for ownership stake in the company through stock options or membership interests," Bryan shared.

"How many things should I ask for during a six month evaluation period?" Paige questioned.

Bryan scratched the side of his face, "Hmm… good question. I personally wouldn't ask for more than two things at once."

"If you presumably have everything you want, you can always ask for new office décor—including furniture, new paint, or new artwork for your office," Bryan claimed. "On the other hand, you can also ask your company to donate a specific amount of money to a charity near and dear to your heart in place of a direct raise."

As the hour drew to a close, Bryan thanked Paige once again for her thoughtful gift. They hugged briefly and he wished her nothing but the best in her current and future endeavors.

Paige could not wait to share her notes with Kerry, Richard, and her Grandpa Bill.

HELPFUL TIPS:

- Read the book *Everybody Wants Your Money: The Straight-Talking Guide to Protecting (and Growing) the Wealth You Worked So Hard to Earn* by David W. Latko.

SUMMARY NOTES:

1. Success means different things to everyone and their definition of success may change to reflect their priorities.
2. Stay positive and humbly ask for help when you experience setbacks along your journey.
3. Perseverance will pay.

It is my prayer that readers of this book were able to find at least one piece of valuable information that they can apply to their personal journey.

Also, I hope my contributions give you the courage to pursue a raise or a promotion.

If and when you DO earn that pay increase or lucrative promotion, consider donating something to a charity of your choice, or reaffirming your dedication to tithing at church. Lastly, save and then invest at least 10% of every paycheck for a rainy day, and invest 10%—50% of every paycheck to plan for retirement.

It is important to sacrifice for a wealthier tomorrow by saving a portion of each paycheck today. True wealth is not in how much you make, but how much you SAVE each and every paycheck.

I would love to hear your feedback and perspectives, along with any positive experiences you have based on my suggestions after finishing this book, so please do not hesitate to reach out to me through email or social media.

Website - www.VonElijah.com

Email - Keeon@VonElijah.com

Pinterest.com/VonElijah
Twitter.com/VonElijahllc
Facebook.com/VonElijahllc
Instagram.com/Von_Elijah

About the Author

A fashion designer with an eye for color coordination, Keeon Rudder founded the company VON ELIJAH which design athletic apparel to help avid gym, crossfit, IFBB pro, and yoga enthusiasts look amazing! His colorful yoga pants, board shorts, and basketball shorts all have pockets that allow consumers to secure their personal belongings with ease.

Rudder, whose also known for his four published books, has garnered multiple patents for his innovative weightlifting glove and reversible umbrella that can open and close on both sides. His design ingenuity is only surpassed by his willingness to lend a helping hand as well as his penchant for providing first class customer service to all of his clients.

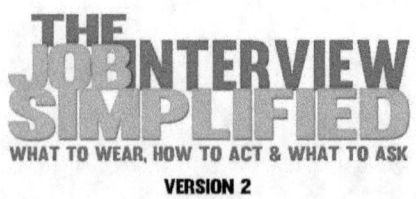

VON ELIJAH Presents:

THE JOB INTERVIEW SIMPLIFIED
WHAT TO WEAR, HOW TO ACT & WHAT TO ASK
VERSION 2

Featuring 60 thought-provoking questions to ask your interviewers.

KEEON RUDDER

The Job Interview Simplified can help job seekers land any job in any industry. It gives men and women simple, straightforward guidelines on applying for a job: resume tips, dining etiquette, how to land an interview, what to wear to an interview, how to act, tips for ex-convicts, email etiquette, how to ace both private and public interviews, and sixty specific questions to ask interviewers.

The Purpose of College Simplified: Options After High School, Obtaining Success & Choosing a Career

will give its readers a clear understanding of the purpose of college so they can be better equipped to decide if college is the right step for them. Readers will also learn how to choose the right college and major, manage stress, get an "A" in every class, meet new people, land internships, employ innovative methods to choosing a career path, learn the specific values that make success at every level attainable, and learn how to increase their revenue stream. Most importantly, the book answers the age old question, "Do I need a college degree to make a good living?"

Acknowledgments

The BIGGEST thank you goes to Melissa Wiggins. You are simply amazing, intelligent, kind, brutally honest, and have the biggest heart. Thank you for making time in your super busy schedule to edit every single one of my books to date. Your advice and candor has served me well. Every one of my manuscripts would be terribly inferior had you not taken the time to render your perspectives. Again, thank you my wonderful friend!

A round of applause goes to Jared Williams and his graphic design company—*DooglesCreativeSolutions.com*. You have been a wonderful friend and helped me with all of my published books. Thank you for walking the walk and leading by example. While others talk about kindness, you take it a step further and lend a helping hand whenever possible. Thank you good sir!

A heartfelt congratulations to my best friend—Marcus Whatley—on your recent promotion and raise!! You are unapologetically chasing your dreams and that is nothing short of commendable. You continue to lend a listening ear whenever needed and use your resources to help countless others along their journey, including myself. Thank you for your friendship, love and support. I am very proud of you and your many accomplishments thus far.

Thank you Ashley Lepa for taking time out of your hectic schedule to edit my book!! Your vast experience and sage suggestions were insightful and quite practical.

And finally, an emotional thanks to my heavenly Father for sticking by my side throughout life's many ups and downs. Thank you for holding every one of my tears in the palm of your hand. Thank you for using my many trials and tribulations to mold my character to be more like yours. Thank you for being my friend, sounding board, and mentor. Thank you for revealing my talents to me and giving me the opportunity to hone my strengths. God, I give you all of my praise and honor, for each of my accomplishments will forever point back to you.

[1] Mark McCormick, *Harvard Business School Goal Story*,
http://www.lifemastering.com/en/harvard_school.html
[2] Saul McLeod, *Forgetting* (2008),
http://www.simplypsychology.org/forgetting.html
[3] Mark Miller, *Chess Not Checkers: Elevate Your Leadership Game* ().
[4] Steven Parton, *The Science of Happiness: Why complaining is literally killing you* (2015),
http://www.curiousapes.com/the-science-of-happiness-why-complaining-is-literally-killing-you/
[5] Mayo Clinic Staff, *Positive thinking: Stop negative self-talk to reduce stress* (),
http://www.mayoclinic.org/healthy-lifestyle/stress-management/in-depth/positive-thinking/art-20043950?pg=1

www.ingramcontent.com/pod-product-compliance
Lightning Source LLC
Chambersburg PA
CBHW060359190526
45169CB00002B/661